Lunch
AROUND
the WORLD

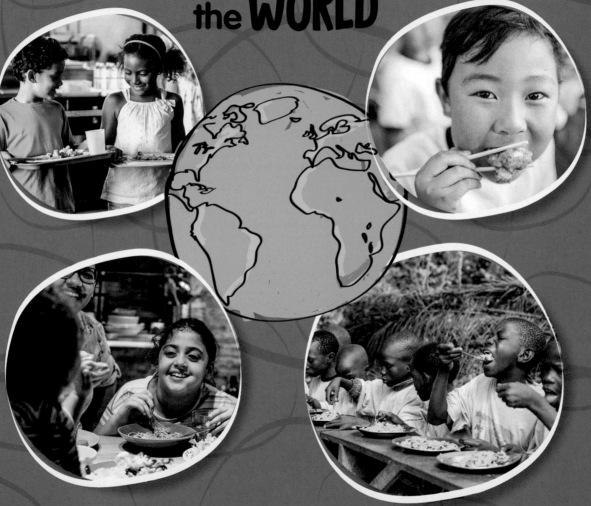

by Jeanette Ferrara

Children's Press®
An imprint of Scholastic Inc.

Library of Congress Cataloging-in-Publication Data
Names: Ferrara, Jeanette, author.
Title: Lunch around the world/Jeanette Ferrara.
Description: First edition. | New York: Children's Press an imprint of Scholastic Inc., 2021. |
    Series: Around the world | Includes index. | Audience: Ages 5–7. | Audience: Grades K–1. |
    Summary: "This book shows the many different ways people eat lunch around the
    world"— Provided by publisher.
Identifiers: LCCN 2021000140 (print) | LCCN 2021000141 (ebook) | ISBN 9781338768671 (library binding) |
    ISBN 9781338768688 (paperback) | ISBN 9781338768695 (ebook)
Subjects: LCSH: Luncheons—Cross-cultural studies—Juvenile literature. | Luncheons—Juvenile
    literature. | Cooking—Juvenile literature.
Classification: LCC TX735 .F47 2021 (print) | LCC TX735 (ebook) | DDC 394.1/253—dc23
LC record available at https://lccn.loc.gov/2021000140
LC ebook record available at https://lccn.loc.gov/2021000141

10 9 8 7 6 5 4 3 2 1   22 23 24 25 26

Printed in Heshan, China 62
First edition, 2022

Series produced by Spooky Cheetah Press
Cover and book design by Kimberly Shake

Photos ©: cover bottom right, 1 bottom right: Egill Bjarnason/Alamy Images; cover top right, 1 top right: Aflo Co., Ltd./Alamy Images; 4 left: Olivier Asselin/Alamy Images; 4 center: Mint Images Limited/Alamy Images; 4 right: Clara Margais/ZUMA Wire/Alamy Images; 5 right: Narinder Nanu/AFP/Getty Images; 6: Mario Fourmy/REA/Redux; 7: Dieter Telemans/Panos Pictures/Redux; 8: François Lochon/Gamma-Rapho/Getty Images; 9: Cavan Images/Alamy Images; 10: Comstock Images/Getty Images; 11: Edwin Remsburg/VW Pics/Getty Images; 12: Maskot/Getty Images; 13: Oleg Bannikov/Dreamstime; 15: Kirk Treakle/Alamy Images; 16: LauriPatterson/Getty Images; 17: Anjum Naveed/AP Images; 18: JohnnyGreig/Getty Images; 19: Robert Convery/Alamy Images; 20: Steve Russell/ZUMAPRESS/Newscom; 21: FatCamera/Getty Images; 22: Dinodia Photos/Alamy Images; 23: Liu Liqun/Getty Images; 24: Asael/Art In All Of Us; 26-27 background: Jim McMahon/Mapman®; 26 top: Glenda Christina/Design Pics/Getty Images; 26 bottom: mother image/Getty Images; 27 top left: Joao Bolan/SOPA Images/LightRocket/Getty Images; 27 bottom: Carolyn Boyd/Alamy Images; 28 left: Novo Image/Glasshouse Images/Newscom; 29 top: Mario Villafuerte/Getty Images; 29 bottom center: Ryman Cabannes/Corinne-Pierre/Getty Images; 31: princessdlaf/Getty Images.

All other photos © Shutterstock.

TABLE of CONTENTS

introduction

JUST LIKE ME

Kids in every country around the world have a lot in common. They go to school and play. They have families and friends. Still, some things—like what they do for lunch—can be very different!

SENEGAL

JAPAN

SPAIN

Lunchtime is a great time to make healthy choices!

INDIA

UNITED STATES

5

chapter 1

LUNCHTIME!

How much time do you have for lunch in school? Some countries have long lunch **periods**. In China, many kids have a two-hour break. They can eat lunch and relax before afternoon class. But the school day in China can be almost 10 hours long! In Spain, some students have a three-hour lunch break!

Only about 20 percent of students in Spain eat lunch at school. The rest go home for lunch.

In China, a hearty lunch of rice and tofu gives kids the energy they need to get through a long day.

These South Korean students are enjoying sushi for lunch.

Kids in other countries are not as lucky! In many South Korean schools, lunch is only 50 minutes long. In Mexico, lunch is combined with recess and may be just 30 minutes long. In the United States, students may get as little as 15 minutes for lunch. Talk about fast food!

In Mexico, lunch is a quick snack. Kids eat a larger meal at home after school.

chapter 2

WHAT IS ON THE MENU?

In the United States, many kids buy lunch at school. Schools try to serve **nutritious** lunches. They have to follow strict rules. Each school lunch has to include a fruit, a vegetable, a grain, and a protein. There is also milk to drink.

American schools started serving student lunches in the 1940s.

In the United States, students often wait in a line and get their food on a tray.

Today's Pears are from Lewis Orchards Smithsburg, Maryland

Today's Tomatoes are from the Sunny Meadows Farm Boonsboro, Maryland

Today's Squash & Zucchini is from the Houser Farm Williamsport, Maryland

Many schools in Belgium serve fruits and vegetables from nearby farms.

Some schools in Belgium serve lunch family-style. The students sit together at a large table. The meal is placed in the center of the table, and students serve themselves. Lunch at a Belgian school usually includes a hot dish, fresh fruit, and salad.

Vegetable **casserole** is a popular dish in Belgium's schools.

In Japan, many elementary and middle school students are not allowed to bring lunch from home. They eat their meals in the classroom with their teachers. Traditional foods like rice and meat **curry** are popular. In South Africa, hearty homemade stews full of vegetables, meat, potatoes, and **spices** are popular. After the students eat, they wash their own dishes.

These South African students are having potjiekos (poi-KEY-kos). The stew is named for the pot it's cooked in!

In Japan, some students serve each other lunch.

chapter 3
PACKED LUNCHES

Some kids bring their lunch from home. In Pakistan, many kids bring a bagged lunch to school. They often have leftovers from last night's dinner. School leaders check to make sure the kids' lunches are healthy. Students are not allowed to have candy or chips!

Many kids in Pakistan enjoy chicken kebab sandwiches.

These students in Pakistan wear aprons during lunch to keep their uniforms clean.

17

More schools in New Zealand are starting to provide lunch. Kids still sit outside, though!

Some schools in New Zealand don't have kitchens or **cafeterias**. Many kids bring their lunches and eat picnic-style outside. Handheld foods like Marmite sandwiches and veggie sticks are popular. Students also have a midmorning snack break. They munch on healthy snacks like fresh fruit.

Marmite is a sticky brown spread. It has a salty flavor.

Canada is another country where most schools don't have kitchens. Students bring healthy lunches from home. Kids are asked to use **reusable** containers. That helps reduce waste. Reducing waste helps protect the **environment**.

A reusable container can mean a litter-free lunch.

In Canada, elementary school children eat together in their classroom.

21

chapter 4

HOME COOKING

Many students eat lunch at home. In Mongolia, some students have class only in the morning. Others have class only in the afternoon. Lunch is eaten with the family, and often starts with a cup of tea. In India, many children take their lunch break at home with their families. They often eat a big meal of curry, rice, and yogurt.

In India, families often sit on the floor to eat.

Some people in Mongolia add a bit of butter to their tea.

In Brazil, school ends at lunchtime. Kids eat at home with their families. Students in Mali go to class in the morning. They head home for several hours to eat lunch. Then they go back to school until 5:00 in the evening.

You have explored many different lunch routines, from breaks that last 15 minutes or 3 hours to meals that are carried in a bag or served by friends. How do they compare to yours?

Kids in Mali can buy a snack of fresh doughnuts on their way home from school.

In Brazil, lunch is the biggest meal of the day.

25

IF YOU LIVED HERE . . .

Let's take a look at more lunch routines
around the world!

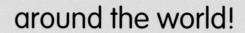

UNITED STATES
In Alaska, schools try
to serve food from
local farmers.

BARBADOS
Lunch is often free—and
so is the morning snack
of milk and cookies!

SOUTH KOREA

Lunch is served on metal trays. The rice is on the left, and the soup is on the right.

KENYA

Most students eat a mixture of dried beans and corn for lunch. That is a traditional dish of the Kikuyu people.

ZAMBIA

Students often eat nshima (uhn-SHEE-mah) for lunch. That is a thick cornmeal porridge with relish.

A CLOSER LOOK

Let's take a look at the different lunch snacks
kids enjoy around the world.

Israel

Israeli children love
snacking on fluffy,
eggy challah. This
braided bread is
slightly sweet and
sometimes has dried
fruit and honey inside.

Panama

In Panama, children
keep snacking simple
with chips and salsa.
Crispy fried corn
tortillas and spicy
tomato dip are a
favorite combination.

Nigeria

In Nigeria, students
love snacking on
fried plantains.
Plantains are similar
to bananas, but they
are less sweet and are
meant to be cooked.

Students in the United States drink more than five billion cartons of milk at lunch every year!

Sweden

Crispbread is a popular snack in this country. This cracker-like flatbread can be enjoyed plain or with any kind of topping.

Thailand

Sticky rice pudding served on banana leaves is popular in Thailand. This sweet treat is made from coconut milk, rice, and bananas.

United States

Many kids choose chocolate milk with their lunch for a little treat. Schools serve only low-fat chocolate milk to make the drink healthier.

GLOSSARY

cafeterias (kaf-uh-TEER-ee-uhz) the rooms in schools where meals are served and eaten

casserole (KAS-uh-role) a dish that is cooked slowly in an oven

curry (KUR-ee) a dish made with meat, fish, or vegetables and a powder that has a spicy taste

environment (en-VYE-ruhn-muhnt) the natural surroundings of living things, such as the air, land, and sea

nutritious (noo-TRISH-uhs) containing substances that help you stay healthy and strong

periods (PEER-ee-uhdz) parts of the school day

porridge (POR-ij) a kind of hot cereal made by boiling oats or other grains in milk or water until the mixture is thick

reusable (ree-YOO-zuh-buhl) capable of being used again rather than thrown away

spices (SPY-sez) plant substances with distinctive smells or tastes that are used to flavor food

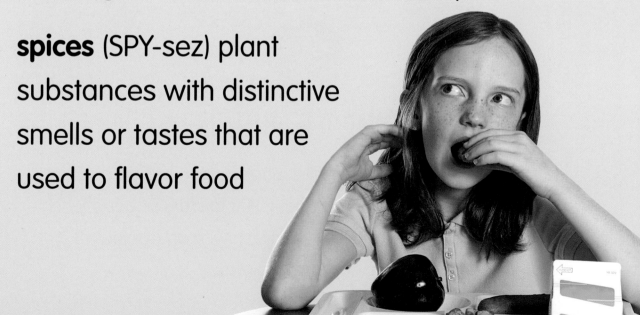

INDEX

ABOUT THE AUTHOR

Jeanette Ferrara is a journalist. She's written hundreds of magazine articles for young readers. Her favorite bagged lunch is a peanut butter and jelly sandwich with an apple and a piece of chocolate.